Communication Strategies

90 Minute Guides

Michelle N. Halsey

Silver City Publications & Training, L.L.C.
P.O. Box 1914
Nampa, ID 83653
https://www.silvercitypublications.com/shop/

ISBN-10: 1-64004-012-9
ISBN-13: 978-1-64004-012-0

Contents

Chapter 1 – The Big Picture

For the better part of every day, we are communicating to and with others. Whether it's the speech you deliver in the boardroom, the level of attention you give your spouse when they are talking to you, or the look that you give to the cat, it all means something. This workshop will help participants understand the different methods of communication and how to make the most of each of them.

By the end of this chapter, you should be able to:

- Understand what communication is

- Identify ways that communication can happen

- Identify barriers to communication and how to overcome them

- Develop their non-verbal and paraverbal communication skills

- Use the STAR method to speak on the spot

- Listen actively and effectively

- Ask good questions

- Use appreciative inquiry as a communication tool

- Adeptly converse and network with others

- Identify and mitigate precipitating factors

- Establish common ground with others

- Use "I" messages

Communication Strategy Activity

Think of a situation where you missed an opportunity because of a lack of communication, and what communication skills in particular could have alleviated the problem. Take some time now to share your thoughts.

When we say the word, "communication," what do you think of? Many people will think of the spoken word. People who are hearing impaired, however, might think of sign language. People who are visually impaired might think of Braille as well as sounds.

In this module, we will explore the different ways in which we communicate.

What is Communication?

The dictionary defines communication as, "the imparting or interchange of thoughts, opinions, or information by speech, writing, or signs."

It is also defined as, "means of sending messages, orders, etc., including telephone, telegraph, radio, and television," and in biology as an, "activity by one organism that changes or has the potential to change the behavior of other organisms."

The effectiveness of your communication can have many different effects on your life, including items such as:

- Level of stress

- Relationships with others

- Level of satisfaction with your life

- Productivity

- Ability to meet your goals and achieve your dreams

- Ability to solve problems

How Do We Communicate?

We communicate in three major ways:

- Spoken: There are two components to spoken communication.

    o Verbal: This is what you are saying.

    o Paraverbal: This means how you say it – your tone, speed, pitch, and volume.

- Non-Verbal: These are the gestures and body language that accompany your words. Some examples: arms folded across your chest, tracing circles in the air, tapping your feet, or having a hunched-over posture.

- Written: Communication can also take place via fax, e-mail, or written word.

Other Factors in Communication

Other communication factors that we need to consider.

- Method: The method in which the communicator shares his or her message is important as it has an effect on the message itself. Communication methods include person-to-person, telephone, e-mail, fax, radio, public presentation, television broadcast, and many more!

- Mass: The number of people receiving the message.

- Audience: The person or people receiving the message affect the message, too. Their understanding of the topic and the way in which they receive the message can affect how it is interpreted and understood.

Chapter 2 – Understanding Communication

On the surface, communication seems pretty simple. I talk, you listen. You send me an e-mail, I read it. Larry King makes a TV show, we watch it.

Like most things in life, however, communication is far more complicated than it seems. Let's look at some of the most common barriers and how to reduce their impact on communication.

An Overview of Common Barriers

Many things can impede communication. Common things that people list as barriers include:

- I can't explain the message to the other person in words that they understand.

- I can't show the other person what I mean.

- I don't have enough time to communicate effectively.

- The person I am trying to communicate with doesn't have the same background as me, and is missing the bigger picture of my message.

These barriers typically break down into three categories: language, culture, and location.

Language Barriers

Of course, one of the biggest barriers to written and spoken communication is language. This can appear in three main forms:

- The people communicating speak different languages.

- The language being used is not the first language for one or more people involved in the communication.

- The people communicating speak the same language, but are from different regions and therefore have different dialects and or unique subtleties.

There are a few ways to reduce the impact of these barriers.

- As a group, identify that the barrier exists. Identify things that the group can do to minimize it.

- Pictures speak a thousand words, and can communicate across languages.

- If you are going to be communicating with this person on a long-term basis, try to find a common language. You may also consider hiring a translator.

Cultural Barriers

There can also be times when people speak the same language, but are from a different culture, where different words or gestures can mean different things. Or, perhaps the person you are communicating with is from a different class from you, or has a very different lifestyle. All of these things can hinder your ability to get your message across effectively.

If you have the opportunity to prepare, find out as much as you can about the other person's culture and background, and how it differs from yours. Try to identify possible areas of misunderstanding and how to prevent or resolve those problems.

An example: A British restaurant owner needs to talk to a culinary specialist in Australia. Although they speak the same language, their words could mean very different things.

If you don't have time to prepare, and find yourself in an awkward situation, use the cultural differences to your advantage. Ask about the differences that you notice, and encourage questions about your culture. Ensure that your questions are curious, not judgmental, resentful, or otherwise negative.

Differences in Time and Place

The last barrier that we will look at is location, definable by time and by place. These barriers often occur when people are in different time zones, or different places.

Take this scenario as an example. Bill works on the east coast, while his colleague, Joe, works on the west coast. Four hours separate their offices. One day, right after lunch, Bill calls Joe to ask for help with a question. Bill has been at work for over four hours already; he is bright, chipper, and in the groove.

Joe, however, has just gotten to the office and is, in fact, running late. He does not feel awake and chipper, and is therefore perhaps not as responsive and helpful in answering Bill's question as he normally is.

Bill thinks, "Geez, what did I do to make Joe cranky?" In response to the way he perceives Joe's behavior, he, too, stops communicating. Their effort to solve a problem together has failed.

So how can you get over the challenges of time and place? First, identify that there is a difference in time and place. Next, try these tips to reduce its impact.

- Make small talk about the weather in your respective regions. This will help you get a picture of the person's physical environment.

- Try to set up phone calls and meetings at a time that is convenient for you both.

- If appropriate, e-mail can be an "anytime, anywhere" bridge. For example, if Bill had sent Joe an e-mail describing the problem, Joe could have addressed it at a better time for him, such as later on in the day. Clearly, this is not always practical (for example, if the problem is urgent, or if it is a complicated issue that requires extensive explanation), but this option should be considered.

Another thing to watch out for is rushed communication. The pressure of time can cause either party to make assumptions and leaps of faith. Always make sure you communicate as clearly as possible, and ask for playback. The listening and questioning skills that you will learn in this workshop will help you make the most of the communication time that you do have.

Para Verbal Communication Skills

Have you ever heard the saying, "It's not what you say, it's how you say it"? It's true!

Try saying these three sentences out loud, placing the emphasis on the underlined word.

- "I didn't say you were wrong." (Implying it wasn't me)

- "I didn't say you were wrong." (Implying I communicated it in another way)

- "I didn't say you were wrong." (Implying I said something else)

Now, let's look at the three parts of paraverbal communication; which is the message told through the pitch, tone, and speed of our words when we communicate.

The Power of Pitch

Pitch can be most simply defined as the key of your voice. A high pitch is often interpreted as anxious or upset. A low pitch sounds more serious and authoritative. People will pick up on the pitch of your voice and react to it. As well, variation in the pitch of your voice is important to keep the other party interested.

If you naturally speak in a very high-pitched or low-pitched voice, work on varying your pitch to encompass all ranges of your vocal cords. (One easy way to do this is to relax your throat when speaking.) Make sure to pay attention to your body when doing this – you don't want to damage your vocal cords.

The Truth about Tone

Did your mother ever say to you, "I don't like that tone!" She was referring to the combination of various pitches to create a mood. (Speed, which we will discuss in the next module, can also have an effect on your tone.)

Here are some tips on creating a positive, authoritative tone.

- Try lowering the pitch of your voice a bit.

- Smile! This will warm up anyone's voice.

- Sit up straight and listen.

- Monitor your inner monologue. Negative thinking will seep into the tone of your voice.

The Strength of Speed

The pace at which you speak also has a tremendous effect on your communication ability. From a practical perspective, someone who speaks quickly is harder to understand than someone who speaks at a moderate pace. Conversely, someone who speaks v-e---r----y s---l-----o---w---l---y will probably lose their audience's interest before they get very far!

Speed also has an effect on the tone and emotional quality of your message. A hurried pace can make the listener feel anxious and rushed. A slow pace can make the listener feel as though your message is not important. A moderate pace will seem natural, and will help the listener focus on your message.

One easy way to check your pitch, tone, and speed is to record yourself speaking. Think of how you would feel listening to your own voice. Work on speaking the way you would like to be spoken to.

Non-Verbal Communication

When you are communicating, your body is sending a message that is as powerful as your words.

In our following discussions, remember that our interpretations are just that – common interpretations. (For example, the person sitting with his or her legs crossed may simply be more comfortable that way, and not feeling closed-minded towards the discussion. Body language can also mean different things across different genders and cultures.) However, it is good to understand how various behaviors are often seen, so that we can make sure our body is sending the same message as our mouth.

Think about these scenarios for a moment. What non-verbal messages might you receive in each scenario? How might these non-verbal messages affect the verbal message?

- Your boss asks you to come into his office to discuss a new project. He looks stern and his arms are crossed.

- A team member tells you they have bad news, but they are smiling as they say it.

- You tell a co-worker that you cannot help them with a project. They say that it's OK, but they slam your office door on their way out.

This is the first goal of this module: to help you understand how to use body language to become a more effective communicator. Another goal, one which you will achieve with time and practice, is to be able to interpret body language, add it to the message you are receiving, and understand the message being sent appropriately.

With this in mind, let's look at the components of non-verbal communication.

Understanding the Mehrabian Study

In 1971, psychologist Albert Mehrabian published a famous study called <u>Silent Messages</u>. In it, he made several conclusions about the way the spoken word is received. Although this study has been misquoted often throughout the years, its basic conclusion is that 7% of our message is verbal, 38% is paraverbal, and 55% is from body language.

Now, we know this is not true in all situations. If someone is speaking to you in a foreign language, you cannot understand 93% of what they are saying. Or, if you are reading a written letter, you are likely getting more than 7% of the sender's message.

What this study does tell us is that body language is a vital part of our communication with others. With this in mind, let's look at the messages that our body can send.

Chapter 3 – All About Body Language

Body language is a very broad term that simply means the way in which our body speaks to others. We have included an overview of three major categories below; we will discuss a fourth category, gestures, in a moment.

The way that we are standing or sitting

Think for a moment about different types of posture and the message that they relay.

- Sitting hunched over typically indicates stress or discomfort.

- Leaning back when standing or sitting indicates a casual and relaxed demeanor.

- Standing ramrod straight typically indicates stiffness and anxiety.

The position of our arms, legs, feet, and hands

- Crossed arms and legs often indicate a closed mind.

- Fidgeting is usually a sign of boredom or nervousness.

Facial expressions

- Smiles and frowns speak a million words.

- A raised eyebrow can mean inquisitiveness, curiosity, or disbelief.

Chewing one's lips can indicate thinking, or it can be a sign of boredom, anxiety, or nervousness.

Interpreting Gestures

A gesture is a non-verbal message that is made with a specific part of the body. Gestures differ greatly from region to region, and from culture to culture. Below we have included a brief list of gestures and their common interpretation in North America.

Gesture	Interpretation
Nodding head	Yes
Shaking head	No

Moving head from side to side	Maybe
Shrugging shoulders	Not sure; I don't know
Crossed arms	Defensive
Tapping hands or fingers	Bored, anxious, nervous
Shaking index finger	Angry
Thumbs up	Agreement, OK
Thumbs down	Disagreement, not OK
Pointing index finger at someone/something	Indicating, blaming
Pointing middle finger (vertically)	Vulgar expression
Handshake	Welcome, introduction
Flap of the hand	Doesn't matter, go ahead
Waving hand	Hello
Waving both hands over head	Help, attention
Crossed legs or ankles	Defensive
Tapping toes or feet	Bored, anxious, nervous

What other gestures can you add to the list?

Speaking Like a STAR

Now that we have explored all the quasi-verbal elements of communication, let's look at the actual message you are sending. You can ensure any message is clear, complete, correct, and concise, with the STAR acronym.

This module will explore the STAR acronym in conjunction with the six roots of open questions (Who? What? When? Where? Why? How?), which will be explored in more detail later on in the workshop.

S = Situation

First, state what the situation is. Try to make this no longer than one sentence. If you are having trouble, ask yourself, "Where?", "Who?", and, "When?". This will provide a base for message so it can be clear and concise.

Example: "On Tuesday, I was in a director's meeting at the main plant."

16

T = Task

Next, briefly state what your task was. Again, this should be no longer than one sentence. Use the question, "What?" to frame your sentence, and add the "Why?" if appropriate.

Example: "I was asked to present last year's sales figures to the group."

A = Action

Now, state what you did to resolve the problem in one sentence. Use the question, "How?" to frame this part of the statement. The Action part will provide a solid description and state the precise actions that will resolve any issues.

Example: "I pulled out my laptop, fired up PowerPoint, and presented my slide show."

R = Result

Last, state what the result was. This will often use a combination of the six roots. Again, a precise short description of the results that come about from your previous steps will finish on a strong definite note.

Example: "Everyone was wowed by my prep work, and by our great figures!"

Let's look at a complete example using STAR. Let's say you're out with friends on the weekend. Someone asks you what the highlight of your week at work was. As it happens, you had a great week, and there is a lot to talk about. You use STAR to focus your answer so you don't bore your friends, and so that you send a clear message.

You respond: "On Tuesday, I was in a director's meeting at the main plant. I was asked to present last year's sales figures to the group. I pulled out my laptop, fired up PowerPoint, and presented my slide show. Everyone was wowed by my prep work, and by our great figures!"

This format can be compressed for quick conversations, or expanded for lengthy presentations. We encourage you to try framing statements with STAR, and see how much more confident you feel when communicating.

Chapter 4 – Listening Skills

So far, we have discussed all the components of sending a message: non-verbal, para-verbal, and verbal. Now, let's turn the tables and look at how to effectively receive messages.

Seven Ways to Listen Better Today

Hearing is easy! For most of us, our body does the work by interpreting the sounds that we hear into words. Listening, however, is far more difficult. Listening is the process of looking at the words and the other factors around the words (such as our non-verbal communication), and then interpreting the entire message.

Let's start out slowly. Here are seven things that you can do to start becoming a better listener right now. Pick a few of them and write them in your action plan.

1. When you're listening, listen. Don't talk on the phone, text message, clean off your desk, or do anything else.

2. Avoid interruptions. If you think of something that needs to be done, make a mental or written note of it and forget about it until the conversation is over.

3. Aim to spend at least 90% of your time listening and less than 10% of your time talking.

4. When you do talk, make sure it's related to what the other person is saying. Questions to clarify expand, and probe for more information will be key tools. (We'll look at questioning skills later on in the workshop.)

5. Do not offer advice unless the other person asks you for it. If you are not sure what they want, ask!

6. Make sure the physical environment is conducive to listening. Try to reduce noise and distractions. ("Would you mind stepping into my office where I can hear you better?" is a great line to use.) If possible, be seated comfortably. Be close enough to the person so that you can hear them, but not too close to make them uncomfortable.

7. If it is a conversation where you are required to take notes, try not to let the note-taking disturb the flow of the conversation. If you need a moment to catch up, choose an appropriate moment to ask for a break.

Understanding Active Listening

Although hearing is a passive activity, one must listen actively to listen effectively, and to actually hear what is being said.

There are three basic steps to actively listening.

1. Try to identify where the other person is coming from. This concept is also called the frame of reference. For example, your reaction to a bear will be very different if you're viewing it in a zoo, or from your tent at a campsite. Your approach to someone talking about a sick relative will differ depending on their relationship with that person.

2. Listen to what is being said closely and attentively.

3. Respond appropriately, either non-verbally (such as a nod to indicate you are listening), with a question (to ask for clarification), or by paraphrasing. Note that paraphrasing does not mean repeating the speaker's words back to them like a parrot. It does mean repeating what you think the speaker said in your own words. Some examples: "It sounds like that made you angry," or, "It sounds like that cashier wasn't very nice to you." (Using the "It sounds like…" precursor, or something similar, gives the speaker the opportunity to correct you if your interpretation is wrong."

Sending Good Signals to Others

When we are listening to others speak, there are three kinds of cues that we can give the other person. Using the right kind of cue at the right time is crucial for keeping good communication going.

• Non-Verbal: As shown in the Mehrabian study, body language plays an important part in our communications with others. Head nods and an interested facial expression will show the speaker that you are listening.

- Quasi-Verbal: Fillers words like, "uh-huh," and "mm-hmmm," show the speaker that you are awake and interested in the conversation.

- Verbal: Asking open questions using the six roots discussed earlier (who, what, where, when, why, how), paraphrasing, and asking summary questions, are all key tools for active listening. (We will look at questioning skills in a moment.)

These cues should be used as part of active listening. Inserting an occasional, "uh-huh," during a conversation may fool the person that you are communicating with in the short term, but you're fooling yourself if you feel that this is an effective communication approach.

Asking Good Questions

Good questioning skills are another building block of successful communication. We have already encountered several possible scenarios where questions helped us gather information, clarify facts, and communicate with others. In this module, we will look closer at these questioning techniques that you can use throughout the communication process.

Open Questions

We discussed open questions a bit when exploring the STAR model earlier. Open questions get their name because the response is open-ended; the answerer has a wide range of options to choose from when answering it.

Open questions use one of six words as a root:

- Who?

- What?

- Where?

- When?

- Why?

- How?

Open questions are like going fishing with a net – you never know what you're going to get! Open questions are great conversation starters, fact finders, and communication enhancers. Use them whenever possible.

Closed Questions

Closed questions are the opposite of open questions; their very structure limits the answer to yes or no, or a specific piece of information. Some examples include:

- Do you like chocolate?

- Were you born in December?

- Is it five o'clock yet?

Although closed questions tend to shut down communication, they can be useful if you are searching for a particular piece of information, or winding a conversation down.

If you use a closed question and it shuts down the conversation, simply use an open-ended question to get things started again. Here is an example:

- Do you like the Flaming Ducks hockey team?

- Yes.

- Who is your favorite player?

Probing Questions

In addition to the basic open and closed questions, there is also a toolbox of probing questions that we can use. These questions can be open or closed, but each type serves a specific purpose.

Clarification

By probing for clarification, you invite the other person to share more information so that you can fully understand their message. Clarification questions often look like this:

- "Please tell me more about…"

- "What did you mean by…"

- "What does … look like?" (Any of the five senses can be used here)

Completeness and Correctness

These types of questions can help you ensure you have the full, true story. Having all the facts, in turn, can protect you from assuming and jumping to conclusions – two fatal barriers to communication.

Some examples of these questions include:

- "What else happened after that?"

- "Did that end the …"

Determining Relevance

This category will help you determine how or if a particular point is related to the conversation at hand. It can also help you get the speaker back on track from a tangent.

Some good ways to frame relevance questions are:

- "How is that like…"

- "How does that relate to…"

Drilling Down

Use these types of questions to nail down vague statements. Useful helpers include:

- "Describe…"

- "What do you mean by…?"

- "Could you please give an example?"

Summarizing

These questions are framed more like a statement. They pull together all the relevant points. They can be used to confirm to the listener that you heard what was said, and to give them an opportunity to correct any misunderstandings.

Example: "So you picked out a dress, had to get it fitted three times, and missed the wedding in the end?"

Be careful not to avoid repeating the speaker's words back to them like a parrot. Remember, paraphrasing means repeating what you think the speaker said in your own words.

Chapter 5 – Appreciative Inquiry

Traditional communication often focuses on what is wrong and how we can fix it. Think back to your last performance review, visit to the doctor, or your latest disagreement with a friend or spouse.

Appreciative inquiry does the opposite: it focuses on what is right and how we can make it better. Many organizations have found it to be a refreshing, energizing way of approaching problems and revitalizing their people.

Although we could spend a whole day talking about appreciative inquiry, this module will give you a brief taste of what AI is all about.

The Purpose of AI

To understand the purpose of Appreciative Inquiry, let's look at each of its parts.

- Appreciate is defined by the Random House dictionary as, "to value or regard highly; to be fully conscious of; be aware of; detect; to rise in value."

- In the same dictionary, inquiry is defined as, "the act of inquiring or of seeking information by questioning."

Therefore, appreciative inquiry can be defined as, "the act of seeking information about the things that we value."

The Four Stages

Appreciative Inquiry includes four basic stages. Note that these stages are viewed as a cycle – AI allows people and organizations to grow and evolve through the continuous use of the process.

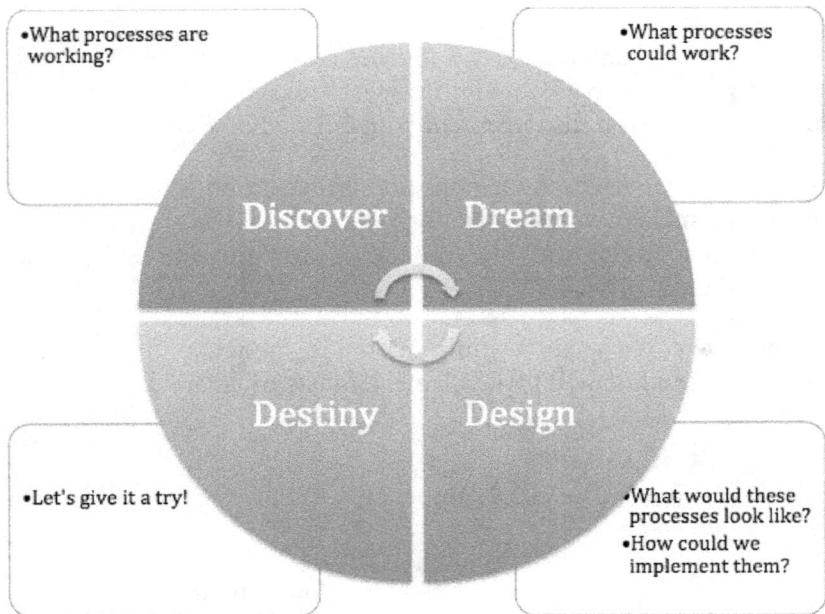

Examples and Case Studies

Appreciative inquiry has been used in many different ways in many different organizations. Some projects where it has been a key tool include:

- Creation of learning network for organizational psychologists at the California School of Professional Psychology

- Process improvement at John Deere that resulted in millions of dollars in savings

- Relief efforts for children orphaned by AIDS in Zimbabwe.

- Integration of mental health services in England.

Chapter 6 – Mastering the Art of Conversation

Engaging in interesting, memorable small talk is a daunting task for most people. How do you know what to share and when to share it? How do you know what topics to avoid? How do you become an engaging converser?

Most experts propose a simple three-level framework that you can use to master the art of conversation. Identifying where you are and where you should be is not always easy, but having an objective outline can help you stay out of sticky situations. We will also share some handy networking tips that will help you get conversations started.

Level One: Discussing General Topics

At the most basic level, stick to general topics: the weather, sports, non-controversial world events, movies, and books. This is typically what people refer to when they say, "small talk."

At this stage, you will focus on facts rather than feelings, ideas, and perspectives. Death, religion, and politics are absolute no-no's. (The exception is when you know someone has had an illness or death in the family and wish to express condolences. In this situation, keep your condolences sincere, brief, and to the point.)

If someone shares a fact that you feel is not true, try to refrain from pointing out the discrepancy. If you are asked about the fact, it's OK simply to say, "I wasn't aware of that," or make some other neutral comment.

Right now, you are simply getting to know the other party. Keep an eye out for common ground while you are communicating. Use open-ended questions and listening skills to get as much out of the conversation as possible.

Level Two: Sharing Ideas and Perspectives

If the first level of conversation goes well, the parties should feel comfortable with each other and have identified some common ground. Now it's time to move a bit beyond general facts and share different ideas and perspectives.

It is important to note that not all personal experiences are appropriate to share at this level. For example, it is fine to share that you like cross-country skiing and went to Europe, but you may not want to share the fact that you took out a personal loan to do so.

Although this level of conversation is the one most often used, and is the most conducive to relationship building and opening communication channels, make sure that you don't limit yourself to one person in a large social gathering. We'll offer some ways to mingle successfully in a few moments.

Level Three: Sharing Personal Experiences

This is the most personal level of conversation. This is where everything is on the table and personal details are being shared. This level is typically not appropriate for a social, casual meeting. However, all of the skills that we have learned today are crucial at this stage in particular: when people are talking about matters of the heart, they require our complete attention, excellent listening skills, and skilled probing with appropriate questions.

Our Top Networking Tips

Understanding how to converse and how to make small talk are great skills, but how do you get to that point? The answer is simple, but far from easy: you walk up, shake their hand, and say hello!

If you're in the middle of a social gathering, try these networking tips to maximize your impact and minimize your nerves.

- Before the gathering, imagine the absolute worst that could happen and how likely it is. For example, you may fear that people will laugh at you when you try to join their group or introduce yourself. Is this likely? At most business gatherings, it's very unlikely!

- Remember that everyone is as nervous as you are. Focus on turning that energy into a positive force.

- To increase your confidence, prepare a great introduction. The best format is to say your name, your organization and/or position title (if appropriate), and something interesting about yourself, or something positive about the gathering. Example: "I'm Tim from Accounting. I think I recognize some of you from the IT conference last month."

- Just do it! The longer you think about meeting new people, the harder it will be. Get out there, introduce yourself, and meet new people.

- Act as the host or hostess. By asking others if they need food or drink, you are shifting the attention from you to them.

- Start a competition with a friend: see how many people each of you can meet before the gathering is over. Make sure your meetings are worthwhile!

- Join a group of odd-numbered people.

- Try to mingle as much as possible. When you get comfortable with a group of people, move on to a new group.

- When you hear someone's name, repeat the introduction in your head. Then, when someone new joins the group, introduce them to everyone.

- Mnemonics are a great way to remember names. Just remember to keep them to yourself! Some examples:

  o Mr. Singh likes to sing.

  o Sue sues people for a living.

  o How funny – Amy Pipes is a plumber!

Chapter 7 – Advanced Communication Skills

We have learned a lot about communication. We would like to wrap things up with a brief discussion on a few advanced communication topics. Adding these skills to your toolbox and using them regularly will make you a more efficient, effective, communicator.

Understanding Precipitating Factors

For many people, life is like a snowball. On a particularly good day, everything may go your way and make you feel like you're on top of the world. But on a bad day, unfortunate events can likewise snowball, increasing their negative effect exponentially.

For example, imagine how each of these events would make you feel if they happened to you first thing in the morning.

- You encounter construction on the way to work.

- Your alarm clock doesn't go off and you wake up late.

- You are out of coffee.

- The cafeteria line is very long.

Each of those things is potentially responsible for creating a crummy morning. Now, imagine this scenario:

You wake up and realize your alarm clock hasn't gone off and you're already late. You get up and go to turn the coffee pot on, but you realize that there is no coffee left in your house. Then, you shower and head out the door – only to encounter construction and massive traffic back-ups on the way to work. Now you're 15 minutes late instead of five. You get to work and head to the cafeteria for some much-needed coffee, but the line stretches out the door.

With the addition of each event, your morning just gets worse and worse. For most people, this is a recipe for disaster – the first person that crosses them is likely to get an earful!

Successful communicators are excellent at identifying precipitating factors and adjusting their approach before the communication starts, or during it. Understanding the power of precipitating factors can also help you de-personalize negative comments. This does not mean that someone having a bad day gets to dump on everyone around them; it does mean, however, that the person being dumped on can take it less personally and help the other person work through their problems.

Establishing Common Ground

Finding common ties can be a powerful communication tool. Think of those times when a stranger turns out not to be a stranger – that the person next to you on the train grew up in the same town that you did, or that the co-worker you never really liked enjoys woodworking as much as you do.

Whenever you are communicating with someone, whether it is a basic conversation, a problem-solving session, or a team meeting, try to find ways in which you are alike. Focusing on positive connections will help you build stronger relationships and better communication.

Using "I" Messages

Framing your message appropriately can greatly increase the power of your communication.

How would you react to these statements?

- Your outfit is too casual for this meeting.

- You mumble all the time.

- You're really disorganized.

Most people would feel insulted and criticized by these statements – and rightly so! They are framed in a way that puts blame on the receiver. These statements can even give the impression that the speaker feels superior to the receiver.

Instead of starting a sentence with "you," try using the "I message" instead for feedback. This format places the responsibility with the speaker, makes a clear statement, and offers constructive feedback.

The format has three basic parts:

- Objective description of the behavior

- Effect that the behavior is causing on the speaker

- The speaker's feelings

Here is an example: "Sometimes, you speak in a very low voice. I often have difficulty hearing you when you speak at that volume. It often makes me feel frustrated."

Be careful not to start the sentence with some form of, "When you…" This tends to create feelings of blame and injustice.

Additional Titles

The 90 Minute Guide series of books covers a variety of general business skills and are intended to be completed in 90 minutes or less. It is an effective way for building your skill set and can be used to acquire professional development units needed by project managers and other industries to maintain their certification. For the availability of titles please see

https://www.silvercitypublications.com/shop/.

No. 1 - Appreciative Inquiry

No. 2 - Assertiveness and Self Control

No. 3 - Attention Management

No. 4 - Body Language Basics

No. 5 - Business Acumen

No. 6 - Business and Etiquette

No. 7 - Change Management

No. 8 - Coaching and Mentoring

No. 9 - Communications Strategies

No. 10 - Conflict Resolution

No. 11 - Creative Problem Solving

No. 12 - Delivering Constructive Criticism

No. 13 - Developing Creativity

No. 14 - Developing Emotional Intelligence

No. 15 - Developing Interpersonal Skills

No. 16 - Developing Social Intelligence

No. 17 - Employee Motivation

No. 18 - Facilitation Skills

No. 19 - Goal Setting and Getting Things Done

No. 20 - Knowledge Management Fundamentals

No. 21 - Leadership and Influence

No. 22 - Lean Process and Six Sigma Basics

No. 23 - Managing Anger

No. 24 - Meeting Management

No. 25 - Negotiation Skills

No. 26 - Networking Inside a Company

No. 27 - Networking Outside a Company

No. 28 - Office Politics for Managers

No. 29 - Organizational Skills

No. 30 - Performance Management

No. 31 - Presentation Skills

No. 32 - Public Speaking

No. 33 - Servant Leadership

www.ingramcontent.com/pod-product-compliance
Lightning Source LLC
Chambersburg PA
CBHW060705280326
41933CB00012B/2309